Explore the Solar System

Human Space Exploration

Revised Edition

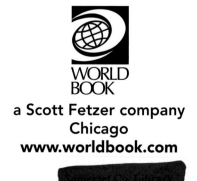

WORLD BOOK

a Scott Fetzer company
Chicago
www.worldbook.com

World Book, Inc.
180 North LaSalle, Suite 900
Chicago, IL 60601
USA

For information about other World Book publications, visit our website at **http://www.worldbook.com** or call **1-800-WORLDBK (967-5325)**.

For information about sales to schools and libraries, call **1-800-975-3250 (United States)**, or **1-800-837-5365 (Canada)**.

Revised printing 2016

The Library of Congress has cataloged an earlier edition of this title as follows:
Human space exploration.
      p. cm. -- (Explore the solar system)
   Summary: "An introduction to human space exploration for primary and intermediate grade students, with information about the early history of space travel and current space exploration. Includes a list of highlights for each chapter, fun facts, glossary, resource list, and index" -- Provided by publisher.
   Includes index.
   ISBN 978-0-7166-9543-1
   1. Space probes--Juvenile literature. 2. Manned space flight--Juvenile literature. 3. Outer space--Exploration--Juvenile literature. I. World Book, Inc.
   TL793.H793 2011
   629.45--dc22
                                          2010009002

This edition:
ISBN: 978-0-7166-2559-9 (print)
Set ISBN 978-0-7166-2549-0 (print)

E-book editions:
ISBN 978-0-7166-1896-6 (EPUB3)
ISBN 978-0-7166-2480-6 (PDF)

Picture Acknowledgments:
Cover front: NASA Human Spaceflight Collection;
Cover back: NASA/JPL-Caltech/UCLA.

© Alamy Images 53; APImages/NASA 15; APWorldwide 57; Bio Serve Space Tech/University of Colorado 27; © Corbis 9, 59; Esther C. Goddard 7; JPL 7; NASA 1, 4, 9, 10, 12, 15, 16, 17, 18, 19, 20, 22, 23, 24, 27, 29, 31, 32, 33, 34, 35, 36, 37, 38, 40, 42, 45, 47, 49, 51, 53; NASA/MSFC 43; NASATV 27; © PhotoEdit 54; Scaled Composites 57; Shutterstock 53; U.S. Navy 41.

Astronomers use different kinds of photos to learn about such objects in space as planets. Many photos show an object's natural color. Other photos use false colors. Some false-color images show types of light the human eye cannot normally see. Others have colors that were changed to highlight important features. When appropriate, the captions in this book state whether a photo uses natural or false color.

Staff

Executive Committee
President: Jim O'Rourke
Vice President and Editor in Chief: Paul A. Kobasa
Vice President, Finance: Donald D. Keller
Vice President, Marketing: Jean Lin
Vice President, International: Kristin Norell
Director, Human Resources: Bev Ecker

Editorial
Manager, Annuals/Series Nonfiction:
   Christine Sullivan
Manager, Science: Jeff De La Rosa
Editor, Science: Will Adams
Administrative Assistant: Ethel Matthews
Manager, Contracts & Compliance
   (Rights & Permissions): Loranne K. Shields
Manager, Indexing Services: David Pofelski

Digital
Director of Digital Product Content Development:
   Emily Kline
Director of Digital Product Development:
   Erika Meller
Digital Product Manager: Lyndsie Manusos
Digital Product Coordinator: Matthew Werner

Manufacturing/Production
Manufacturing Manager: Sandra Johnson
Production/Technology Manager: Anne Fritzinger
Proofreader: Nathalie Strassheim

Graphics and Design
Senior Art Director: Tom Evans
Senior Designer: Isaiah Sheppard
Manager, Cartographic Services: Wayne K. Pichler
Senior Cartographer: John M. Rejba

Printed in China by Shenzhen Donnelley Printing Co., Ltd., Guangdong Province
4th printing June 2016

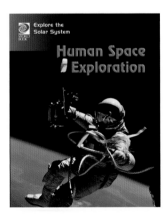

Cover image:
Edward H. White II takes the first spacewalk by an American astronaut, on June 3, 1965, during the Gemini 4 mission.

Contents

Where Does Space Begin? 4

What Were the First Probes Launched into Space? 6

What Was the "Space Race"? 8

What Were the First Piloted Spacecraft Like? 10

What Gives a Spacecraft the Power for Liftoff? 12

Is Space Exploration Dangerous? 14

What Is Microgravity and How Does It Affect Space Travel? 16

Who Were the First People to Travel in Space? 18

Who Was the First Person to Walk in Space? To Walk on the Moon? 20

What Did Astronauts Take from the Moon? Leave on the Moon? 22

Who Were Some Notable Astronauts? .24

What Kinds of Scientific Experiments Have Been Carried Out in Space? . . .26

What Was the Space Shuttle Like? 28

What Do Astronauts Eat in Space? 30

How Do Astronauts Stay Clean in Space? 32

What Do Astronauts Wear on a Space Mission? 34

How Do Astronauts Sleep in Space? 36

What Was the Space Shuttle Used For? 38

What Is Replacing the Space Shuttle? .40

What Will Launch NASA's Orion Capsule into Space? 42

What Is a Space Station? 44

What Is the International Space Station? 46

How Do Astronauts Get to the International Space Station? 48

What Have We Learned So Far on the International Space Station? 50

What Useful Things on Earth Were Created for the Space Program? 52

How Can Kids Get Involved in Space Exploration? 54

Can Tourists Travel into Space? 56

So You Want to Become a Space Explorer? 58

Glossary 60

For More Information 62

Index 63

If a word is printed in **bold letters that look like this,** that word's meaning is given in the glossary on pages 60–61.

Where Does Space Begin?

There is no clear boundary between the **atmosphere** of Earth and outer space. The farther you go from Earth's surface, the thinner the air gets. But most scientists say that outer space begins about 60 miles (95 kilometers) above Earth. Many countries have agreed that the **Karman Line,** an imaginary boundary about 62 miles (100 kilometers) above Earth's surface, is the start of outer space.

When human beings decided to travel into space, they chose Earth's **moon** as the first place to visit. This made sense, because the moon is much closer to Earth than any of the **planets** in the **solar system.** It takes less fuel and time to reach the moon than other objects in space. The moon is about 238,897 miles (384,467 kilometers) from Earth. By comparison, Venus—the planet closest to Earth—is about 23.7 million miles (38.2 million kilometers) away. Neptune, the outermost planet in the solar system, is more than 2.7 billion miles (4.3 billion kilometers) away.

Highlights

- There is no clear boundary between Earth's atmosphere and outer space.
- Most scientists agree that space begins about 60 miles (95 kilometers) above Earth.
- Many countries consider the Karman Line to mark the beginning of outer space.

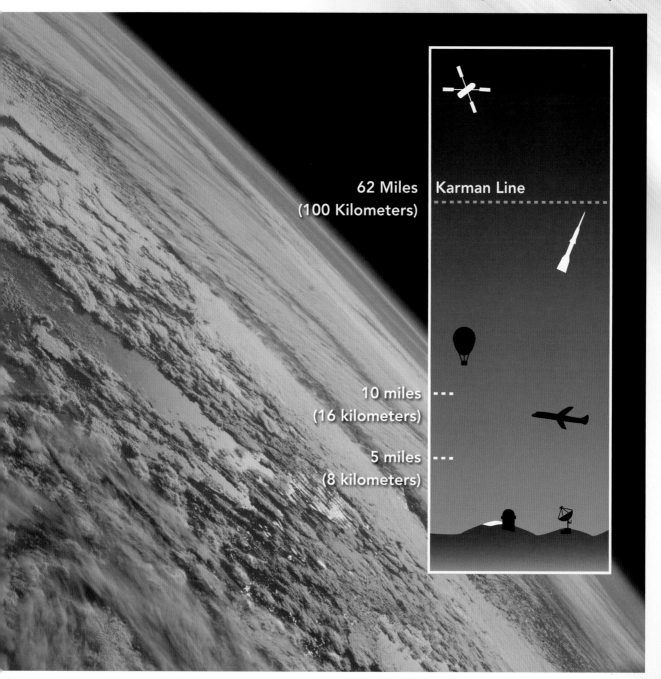

The Karman Line marks the boundary between Earth's atmosphere and outer space.

62 Miles
(100 Kilometers)

Karman Line

10 miles
(16 kilometers)

5 miles
(8 kilometers)

What Were the First Probes Launched into Space?

In the 1930's, scientists began to build and test **rockets** that they hoped would one day be used for space travel. Starting in about 1955, other scientists developed artificial **satellites** that were to be launched into space using rockets.

In 1957, the Soviet Union launched the first artificial satellite. The Soviet Union was a powerful country that existed from 1922 to 1991. The Soviet satellite, called Sputnik (*SPUHT nihk*), had no **astronauts** on board. Unpiloted satellites were a way of learning more about space before sending human beings there. The Soviet Union was also the first country to launch a **probe** to the surface of the **moon.** That probe, Luna 2, was launched in 1959.

Fun Fact

Vanguard I, the first satellite successfully launched by the United States, has been orbiting Earth for more than 50 years since its launch in 1958.

Highlights

- The Soviet Union launched the first artificial satellite, called Sputnik, in 1957.
- The first U.S. satellites to be launched successfully were Explorer 1 and Vanguard 1 in 1958.
- The first probe to the surface of the moon, Luna 2, was launched by the Soviet Union in 1959.

The first satellites that the United States launched successfully were Explorer 1 and Vanguard 1. They were launched in 1958. Vanguard 1 is still in **orbit** today. This satellite has sent a lot of information to Earth. Some of its data proved that Earth is not perfectly round. This information has helped map makers make more accurate world maps.

A team of scientists, including physicist James Van Allen (center) and rocket pioneer Wernher von Braun (right), hold a model of Explorer 1, which was successfully launched on Jan. 31, 1958.

American rocket pioneer Robert H. Goddard (left) and his assistants work on an early rocket in 1940.

What Was the "Space Race"?

In the late 1950's and early 1960's, the United States and the Soviet Union were political rivals. Both countries were working on space exploration programs at that time. The Soviet Union's launch of the **satellite** Sputnik (later called Sputnik 1) in 1957 surprised America. U.S. leaders vowed to do whatever was needed to catch up. This was the start of the **space race.**

Soon after, the U.S. National Aeronautics and Space Administration (NASA) was founded. This agency gathered researchers and laboratories, allowing people to work together toward the goal of space exploration. NASA played a key role in the eventual success of the American space program.

The space race faded by the 1970's, when both the United States and the Soviet Union began to pursue other goals in space. Today, many nations work together on projects in space, including the International Space Station, (ISS—see page 48). Both Russia, which was once part of the Soviet Union, and the United States helped to build the ISS.

Highlights

- The space race was a time of competition between the United States and the Soviet Union over which country would be the first to achieve important goals in exploring outer space.
- The space agency NASA was formed to help the United States achieve its goals.
- Today, many countries work together on space projects.

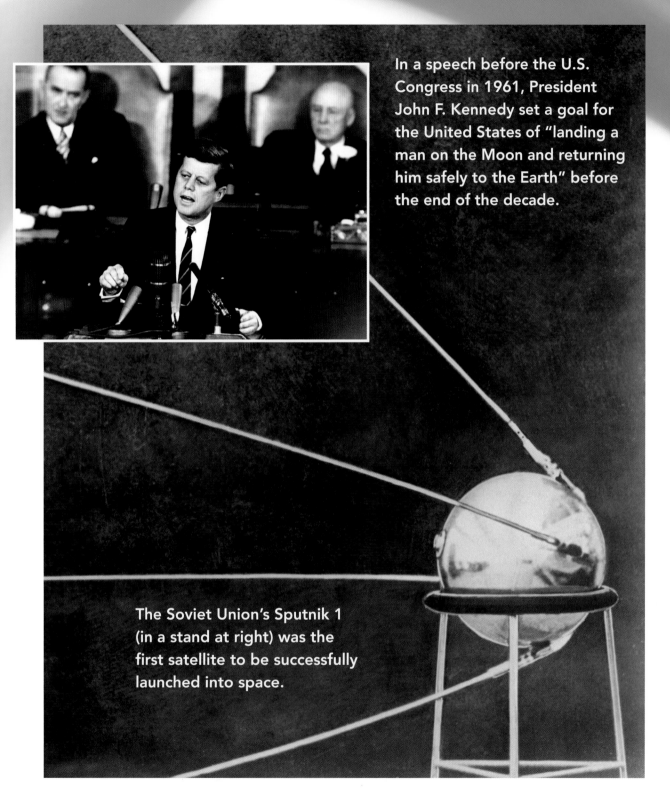

In a speech before the U.S. Congress in 1961, President John F. Kennedy set a goal for the United States of "landing a man on the Moon and returning him safely to the Earth" before the end of the decade.

The Soviet Union's Sputnik 1 (in a stand at right) was the first satellite to be successfully launched into space.

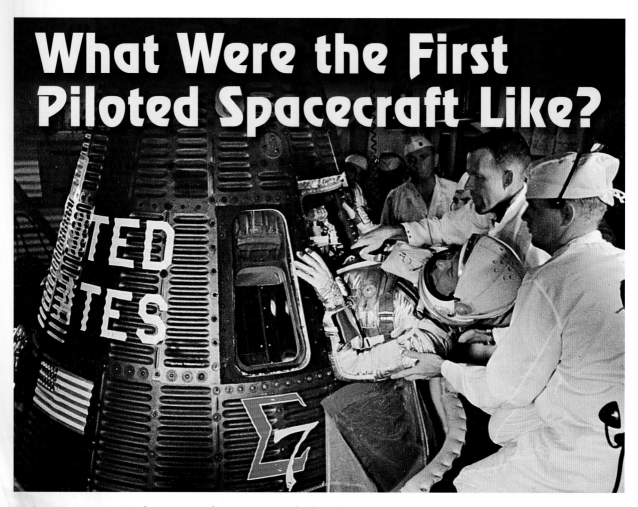

What Were the First Piloted Spacecraft Like?

U.S. astronaut Walter M. Schirra, Jr., is helped into a Mercury capsule before his flight into space in 1962.

The very first piloted spacecraft had room for only one person. That spacecraft was the Soviet Union's Vostok. The Vostok was designed to fall onto land with a parachute. The first type of piloted spacecraft designed by the United States—the Mercury spacecraft—was designed to land in the ocean.

As space programs continued, the **capsules** in which the **astronauts** sat were made bigger so that two or more people could

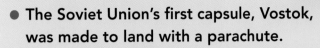

Highlights

- The Soviet Union's first capsule, Vostok, was made to land with a parachute.
- The first U.S. capsule, Mercury, was made to land in the ocean.
- The earliest space capsules carried only one person. Later capsules carried two or more people.

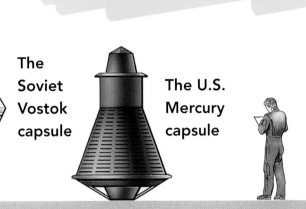

The Soviet Vostok capsule

The U.S. Mercury capsule

stay in space longer. The first spacecraft could stay in space for only about a day. But soon spacecraft could remain in space for up to two weeks.

American spacecraft have sometimes been changed because of comments from the astronauts or experiences during testing and flight. For ex-ample, astronauts asked for a larger window on an early Mercury capsule, and NASA agreed.

The escape **hatch** was also redesigned. In 1967, three astronauts died in a fire on Apollo 1. The capsule's hatch took 90 seconds to open. NASA made a new hatch that could be opened in just a few seconds.

What Gives a Spacecraft the Power for Liftoff?

Overcoming **gravity** is a spacecraft's biggest challenge. A powerful **rocket** called a **launch vehicle** helps a spacecraft overcome gravity and reach space.

Rockets burn either liquid or solid fuel. This fuel is combined with a substance called an oxidizer *(OK suh DY zuhr)*. An oxidizer adds the **oxygen** that fuel needs to burn in space, where there is no air.

Rockets are made up of stages, or sections. Each stage falls away after it is used up, so that the rest of the spacecraft is lighter. Releasing unneeded stages helps the spacecraft use less fuel as it continues in space.

Sometimes rockets called **boosters** are attached to the launch vehicle. Boosters help especially heavy spacecraft overcome gravity.

Highlights

- In order for a spacecraft to lift off, it must overcome the force of gravity.
- Rockets called launch vehicles help spacecraft to lift off.
- Launch vehicles may carry either solid or liquid fuel.
- Large, heavy spacecraft may also need booster rockets.

The space shuttle Discovery is carried into space by a launch vehicle with two boosters. The external tank (orange) is a rocket that carries liquid fuel. The boosters strapped to its sides (only one is visible in the photo) carry solid fuel.

Is Space Exploration Dangerous?

Space exploration has many dangers. Tragic accidents have taken the lives of U.S. **astronauts** as well as **cosmonauts** in the Soviet space program.

Scientists can take action in advance to reduce some of the risks of traveling or living in space. Double *hulls* (the outer walls of a spacecraft) protect against damage caused by *micrometeoroids* (dust particles) and *debris* (space trash). Filters on the windows of a spacecraft protect against damaging **ultraviolet rays** from the sun. Heat shields and a thermal-control system keep people inside the craft safe from the extreme heat and cold of space.

Other risks are harder to predict. Spacecraft are complex vehicles, and it is not always possible to know how something may go wrong. When an explosion occurred on the Apollo 13 spacecraft in 1970, only the fast thinking of the crew in space and NASA scientists on the ground saved the spacecraft and enabled the astronauts to return safely to Earth.

Highlights

- Both U.S. astronauts and Soviet cosmonauts have died during space exploration.
- Scientists who build spacecraft try to make them strong and safe, but sometimes unexpected dangers arise.

Fun Fact

Since 1957, more than 20,000 objects larger than 4 inches (10 centimeters) have become space trash (nonworking objects). These fast-moving objects are a serious danger to spacecraft.

A U.S. naval crew recovers the damaged Apollo 13 spacecraft at sea (above). The bottom of the space shuttle (right) is inspected during each mission for signs of damage to the tiny tiles that protect the spacecraft from the intense heat of launch and landing.

What Is Microgravity and How Does It Affect Space Travel?

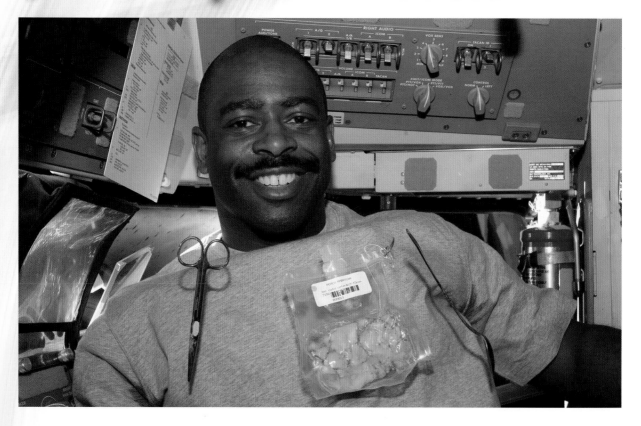

Astronauts are frequently shown floating aboard a spacecraft in what is often called "zero **gravity**" or weightlessness. Zero gravity is actually **microgravity,** a state of extremely low gravity. During space flights, microgravity affects both astronauts and their spacecraft.

U.S. astronaut Leland Melvin aboard the space shuttle Atlantis watches his food, a pair of scissors, and a spoon float by in the microgravity of space.

Microgravity affects the human body in many ways. In the first few days of a mission, about half of all space travelers experience "space sickness." Travelers feel confused—like they are always upside down, no matter which way they turn. They may become sick and vomit. Medicines can help them feel better, and the condition usually goes away after a few days. Other effects on the body include a muscle weakness known as deconditioning.

Microgravity affects a spacecraft just as much as it does the astronauts. In a microgravity environment, fuel does not drain from tanks, so it must be squeezed out by high-pressure gas. Hot air does not rise in microgravity, so fans must be used to circulate the air.

Highlights

- Although many people think there is no gravity in space, there is actually a little gravity, or a state of microgravity.
- Microgravity can make astronauts feel sick in space and make spacecraft harder to operate.
- There are things scientists can do to make astronauts feel better and spacecraft work better in microgravity.

United States astronaut Sandra Magnus exercises aboard the International Space Station to keep her muscles from growing weak while she is in space.

Who Were the First People to Travel in Space?

Soviet cosmonaut Yuri Gagarin travels to the launchpad on April 12, 1961. Gagarin was the first person to travel in space.

Highlights

- Soviet cosmonaut Yuri Gagarin was the first person to travel in space, in April 1961.
- Astronaut Alan B. Shepard, Jr., was the first American to travel in space, in May 1961.
- A dog and a chimpanzee traveled in space even before human beings did.

A **cosmonaut** from the Soviet Union named Yuri Gagarin *(YOOR ee gah GAHR ihn)* was the first person to travel in space. He **orbited** Earth on April 12, 1961, in a trip that lasted 1 hour and 48 minutes. After the flight, he returned safely to Earth.

The first American in space was Alan B. Shepard, Jr. On May 5, 1961, he **rocketed** 117 miles (188 kilometers) into space and landed back on Earth 15 minutes later.

Astronaut Alan B. Shepard, Jr., enters his Mercury capsule as he prepares to become the first American in space.

But even before human beings first explored space, animals traveled on spacecraft. An 11-pound (5-kilogram) dog named Laika *(LY kuh)* was the first space passenger. Laika flew aboard the Soviet craft Sputnik 2 in 1957. Other animal passengers included a chimpanzee named Ham, who made a 16-minute flight in a U.S. Mercury **capsule** in 1961. Over the years, space flights have also included bees, fish, frogs, mice, snails, and other animals.

Who Was the First Person to Walk in Space? To Walk on the Moon?

Soviet **cosmonaut** Alexei Leonov (*uh lyih KSYAY lee OH nohf*) became the first person to step outside a spacecraft and float freely in space. This first **extravehicular activity** took place on March 18, 1965. But the historic event almost ended in disaster. When Leonov tried to get back inside the spacecraft, he found that his spacesuit had *inflated* (filled with air) so much that he could not bend his body to enter the opening to the **airlock.** Finally, he was able to release enough air from his suit to get back onboard Voshkod 2.

United States **astronaut** Neil A. Armstrong was the first person to walk on the surface of the **moon.** After taking the first step on its barren landscape on July 20, 1969, he spoke the now-famous words, "That's one small step for a man, one giant leap for mankind."

Highlights

- Soviet cosmonaut Alexei Leonov was the first person to walk in space, in 1965.
- U.S. astronaut Neil A. Armstrong was the first person to walk on the moon, in 1969.

Neil Armstrong stands beside the lunar module (landing craft) after becoming the first person to walk on the moon. He planted the U.S. flag on the lunar surface.

Cosmonaut Alexei Leonov (in a series of photographs above) became the first person to walk in space.

What Did Astronauts Take from the Moon? Leave on the Moon?

During all six Apollo **moon** landings, **astronauts** collected rock and soil samples to take back to Earth for study. Altogether, astronauts gathered about 840 pounds (384 kilograms) of samples. Some moon rocks are on display in the National Museum of Natural History in Washington, D.C., and in several other U.S. museums. A small number of rocks were given to other countries as goodwill gifts. Most of the

Highlights

- The Apollo astronauts left a flag and a plaque on the moon in 1969.
- Footprints left by astronauts on the moon will probably remain for millions of years.
- Many spacecraft have also been left on the moon, either accidentally or deliberately.

A moon rock brought back by Apollo astronauts

material returned by the Apollo missions is stored in NASA vaults.

Many more objects were left on the moon than were taken away. Astronauts Neil Armstrong and Buzz Aldrin planted a U.S. flag on the moon during their first moonwalk, on July 20, 1969. They also left a plaque. And, of course, all of the astronauts left their footprints. Because there is no wind or water on the moon to disturb them, the footprints should last for millions of years.

The largest objects left on the moon are *stages* (sections) of **rockets** and spacecraft from various countries. These objects either crashed into the moon accidentally or were deliberately crashed during missions exploring the moon. Scientists estimate that about 388,000 pounds (176,000 kilograms) of debris has been left on the moon.

A U.S. flag (above) and a plaque (below) were left on the moon by astronauts Neil Armstrong and Buzz Aldrin in 1969. Their footprints are also visible below the flag.

Who Were Some Notable Astronauts?

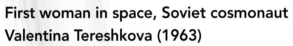

First woman in space, Soviet cosmonaut Valentina Tereshkova (1963)

First Canadian astronaut, Marc Garneau (1984)

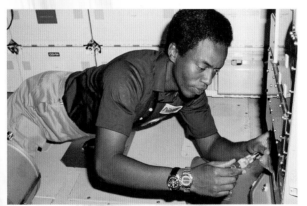

First African-American astronaut, Guion S. Bluford, Jr. (1983)

First Hispanic-American astronaut, Franklin Chang-Diaz (1986)

First American woman in space, astronaut Sally Ride (1983)

First Australian astronaut, Andy Thomas (1996)

People who made history by traveling in space include Valentina Tereshkova (*VAH lehn TEE nah teh rehsh KAW vah*). Tereshkova, a Soviet **cosmonaut,** was the first woman in space. She made the flight in Vostok 6 in June 1963. The first U.S. woman in space was Sally K. Ride. She and four other **astronauts,** made a six-day flight on the space shuttle Challenger in June 1983.

In a flight aboard Challenger, in August 1983, Guion S. Bluford, Jr., became the first African American to go into space. In September 1992, on the space shuttle Endeavour, Mae C. Jemison became the first African American woman to do so.

The youngest astronaut to travel in space was Soviet cosmonaut Gherman Titov (*GUR men TEE tohf*). He was 25 years old when he piloted Vostok 2 in August 1961. The oldest was retired astronaut John H. Glenn, who, in 1998, flew aboard the space shuttle Discovery. Glenn was 77 years old at that time.

The first Canadian in space was Marc Garneau, on the space shuttle Challenger in 1984.

Highlights

- The first women in space were Soviet cosmonaut Valentina Tereshkova in 1963 and American astronaut Sally K. Ride in 1983.
- The youngest astronaut was Soviet cosmonaut Gherman Titov, who was 25. The oldest was retired U.S. astronaut John Glenn, who was 77.

What Kinds of Scientific Experiments Have Been Carried Out in Space?

Many of the experiments performed in space have focused on the effects of **microgravity** on animals, plants, and people. Other experiments have explored the properties of various *materials* (solid forms of matter) in space.

United States scientists began performing experiments in space aboard Skylab, the first American space station. It was in orbit from 1973 to 1979. Spacelab, a reusable laboratory, traveled in the cargo bay of NASA's space shuttles on various missions from 1983 to 1997. There, scientists conducted experiments in such fields as astronomy, biology, and medicine.

Scientists from various nations have also conducted experiments aboard the International Space Station. Sometimes, students are involved in the experiments. In 2008, students compared the lifecycles of butterflies in space with those on Earth.

Highlights

- One of the main types of experiments scientists perform in space is to observe the effects of microgravity on plants, animals, and people.
- Scientists also study whether the properties of various materials change in space.
- Sometimes students participate in space experiments, too.

Astronaut James D. van Hoften
studies a bee experiment aboard
the space shuttle Challenger in 1984.

Orb weaver spiders in an experiment aboard the International Space Station
in 2008 at first were able to weave only a tangled web (below, left). But after
a few days, they became used to the microgravity conditions of space and
wove the symmetrical web they are known for (below, right).

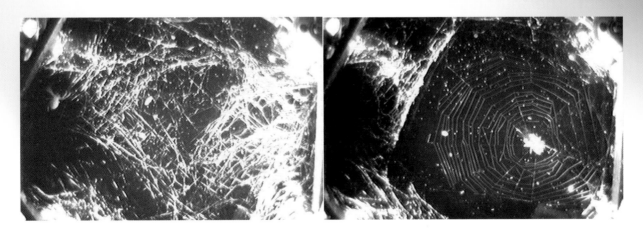

What Was the Space Shuttle Like?

The space shuttle system was made up of three parts: (1) an **orbiter,** (2) an external fuel tank, and (3) two solid rocket **boosters.** The *nose* (front) of the orbiter contained the crew cabin. As many as seven **astronauts** lived and worked in the cabin.

From the **flight deck** at the front of the orbiter, the pilot could look through the front and side windows. The middeck, under the flight deck, had more seats, equipment lockers, sleeping facilities, and a toilet compartment. The shuttle's "kitchen" included hot- and cold-water dispensers, an oven, serving trays for food, and a water heater, but no freezer or refrigerator. The payload bay held the cargo, or goods, hauled by the shuttle. The engines were in the orbiter's tail.

The space shuttle was the first reusable spacecraft. To be reusable, it had to land on solid ground, not water. So the shuttle was designed to take off like a **rocket** but land like an airplane. A heat shield allowed the shuttle to withstand many reentries into Earth's **atmosphere.**

The shuttle flew its first mission in 1981. NASA ended space shuttle missions in 2011.

Highlights

- The space shuttle was the first reusable spacecraft.
- It flew its first mission in 1981.
- NASA ended space shuttle missions in 2011.

Parts of the space shuttle system

Rocket booster

Fuel tank

Rocket booster

Orbiter

USA

United States

NASA
Discovery

The space shuttle Discovery is prepared for launch.

What Do Astronauts Eat in Space?

The food served on a spacecraft has come a long way since the Mercury **astronauts** dined in space. Those early astronauts had to squeeze their semiliquid foods—said to be less than tasty—out of aluminum tubes similar to toothpaste tubes.

Today, astronauts have many choices of things to eat, including macaroni and cheese, beef, peanut butter and jelly, chicken soup, brownies, apples, carrot sticks, and nuts. Some modern meals in space are ready-to-eat. The astronauts have to add water to other foods. Meals can be heated in an on-board oven.

All drinks, even coffee and cocoa, are served in a pouch with

Fun Fact

Astronauts in space eat a lot of wet and sticky foods, such as oatmeal, pudding, and stew. That is because such foods stick to a fork or spoon instead of breaking apart into crumbs and flying off.

a straw or in a squeeze bottle. That is because in **microgravity,** if you tip a cup, the liquid will not move toward your mouth. Instead, it will float away.

In space, astronauts can eat upside down—or at least upside down in relation to the spacecraft. That is because in microgravity, there is no true "up" or "down."

Highlights

- Early astronauts had to squeeze their food out of tubes similar to those that hold toothpaste.

- Today, astronauts have much more variety in their meals.

- Most astronaut meals today are either ready-to-eat or prepared by adding water to them.

- Astronauts must drink all liquids—even coffee and cocoa—through a straw.

Russian cosmonaut Yuri Malenchenko (left) and U.S. astronaut Edward Lu prepare to eat a meal aboard the International Space Station in 2003.

Human Space Exploration **31**

How Do Astronauts Stay Clean in Space?

There was no shower, bathtub, or sink on the space shuttle. Room and water were limited, and water floating around in **microgravity** could damage sensitive equipment. Shuttle **astronauts** "bathed" by rubbing wet cloths over their body, using one for washing and one for rinsing. They washed their hair with rinseless shampoo. They brushed their teeth using toothpaste that can be swallowed or regular toothpaste that is either spit into

Highlights

- Astronauts aboard the space shuttle used washcloths and rinseless shampoo to stay clean.
- Astronauts aboard the space station can bathe in an enclosed, cylindrical shower and then vacuum up the water.

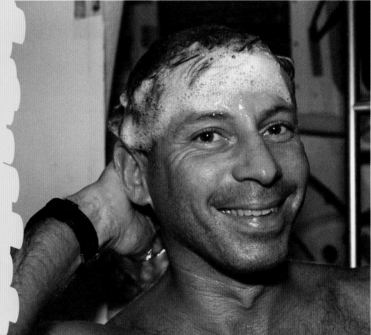

Astronaut Kenneth D. Cockrell washes his hair aboard the space shuttle Columbia. He used a special shampoo that did not need to be rinsed out.

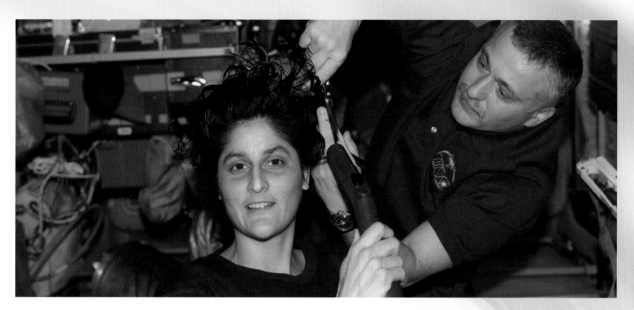

Cosmonaut Fyodor Yurchikhin cuts astronaut Sunita Williams's hair aboard the ISS. Williams holds a vacuum device to capture the bits of cut hair.

tissue or suctioned out, like in a dentist's office.

The International Space Station (ISS) has a *cylindrical* (tall and round) shower stall. Crew members close the door and spray themselves with water. Soap and water stick to the skin because of microgravity. When they are finished, crew members vacuum up the water. NASA's Skylab space station had a similar shower.

Astronauts on the space shuttle and the ISS use toilets that flush with air, not water. The toilets work like vacuum cleaners, with fans that suck air and waste into a storage tank. Astronauts must clamp themselves to the seat while using the toilet, to keep from floating away. In 2008, astronauts began recycling all the water aboard the space station so that it could be reused.

What Do Astronauts Wear on a Space Mission?

Crews on the space shuttle wear special suits for launch and reentry. They wear different suits for **extravehicular activity (EVA),** or work outside the spacecraft or space station. Launch and Entry Suits protect against fire and keep pressure around the **astronauts'** bodies in case the spacecraft's pressurization systems fail. EVA suits act like a self-contained spacecraft to keep the astronaut safe.

On the International Space Station, astronauts wear ordinary shorts or pants, a short- or long-sleeved shirt, and socks. The pants and shorts have plenty of

Astronaut Edward Fincke checks the condition of extravehicular activity (spacewalking) suits aboard the ISS.

A crew aboard the space shuttle Endeavour prepares for lift-off in their Launch and Entry Suits in 2002.

pockets with Velcro closings to secure objects that would otherwise float away. Astronauts wore the same type of clothing inside the shuttle, after launch and before reentry.

Crews on the shuttle carried a change of clothes for each day of the mission. On the ISS, there is no washing machine and little storage space, so astronauts change their shirts and pants about once every three or four days. Dirty clothing is usually placed in an unpiloted, one-way vehicle that has carried supplies to the station. The vehicle is placed on a collision course with Earth and burns up as it reenters Earth's **atmosphere.**

Highlights

- Astronauts wear one type of suit for launch and reentry and another type for spacewalks.
- Aboard the ISS, astronauts wear short- or long-sleeved shirts and pants or shorts with many pockets.

Human Space Exploration 35

How Do Astronauts Sleep in Space?

On the International Space Station, there are small crew cabins, just big enough for one person. Each cabin has a sleeping bag and a window that looks out into space.

On the shuttle, there are no private rooms for crew members. Because of **microgravity**, shuttle **astronauts** could drift around the spacecraft as they sleep. So astronauts use sleeping bags that can be clipped to walls, the ceiling, or a seat. Or, they may decide to sleep strapped into the commander's or pilot's seats.

Astronaut Peggy Whitson slips into a sleeping compartment aboard the International Space Station.

All of these sleep choices prevented astronauts from bumping into one another or into equipment and walls that would wake or injure them. In microgravity, sleeping bags can be attached in any position that is practical. Since there is no "up" in space, the astronauts can sleep just as comfortably positioned *vertically* (up and down) as they can *horizontally* (side to side).

On the shuttle, astronauts could wear sleeping masks at bedtime to block the sunlight that streams in through the windows at times as the spacecraft **orbited** Earth.

A sleeping compartment aboard the ISS has places for astronauts to attach personal photos and their sleeping bag; a shelf or desktop to work on; and netted storage for clothing.

Highlights

- Astronauts aboard the ISS sleep in small individual cabins.
- Astronauts on the space shuttle slept in sleeping bags that could be attached to a wall, the ceiling, or a seat.
- Because of the microgravity environment in space, astronauts can sleep either vertically or horizontally.

What Was the Space Shuttle Used For?

Space shuttles carried artificial **satellites,** space **probes,** and other heavy loads into **orbit** around Earth beginnng in 1981. In addition, shuttle were used to retrieve artificial satellites that needed repair. **Astronauts** aboard the shuttle could fix a satellite and then return it to orbit. Shuttle crews also conducted many kinds of scientific experiments and observations.

In 1993, a crew from the shuttle Endeavour repaired the three-year-old orbiting Hubble Space Telescope. The repairs enabled the telescope to capture and send images in detail never seen before. Shuttles flew four other missions to Hubble over the years, the last one in 2009.

Shuttles also were used to take crews and cargo to and from the International Space Station. The shuttle Endeavour carried Unity, the first U.S.-built section of the space station, into orbit in 1998. The shuttles carried many other pieces of the station into space. They also flew tons of supplies to the astronauts and experiments for scientists to conduct on the ISS.

Highlights

- The space shuttle flew its first mission in 1981.
- Space shuttles flew their last mission in 2011.
- Space shuttles were used to carry heavy objects into space, repair satellites, and conduct experiments in microgravity.

Fun Fact

In 1995, the U.S. space shuttle Atlantis linked up with Russia's space station, Mir, in an historic docking of spacecraft from the two once-competitive nations.

Astronaut F. Story Musgrave rides the space shuttle's robotic arm as he works to repair the Hubble Space Telescope in 1993.

What Is Replacing the Space Shuttle?

The space shuttle was the first spacecraft that was mostly reusable. Even so, each mission cost an estimated $1 billion. In the early 2000's, NASA began to worry about the age and safety of the **orbiters.**

Two shuttle missions ended in disaster. In 1986, the shuttle Challenger broke apart shortly after launch, killing all seven **astronauts** aboard. In 2003, the shuttle Columbia broke apart as it reentered Earth's **atmosphere.** All seven crew members died in this disaster, too. In 2011, NASA ended all shuttle missions.

NASA plans to replace the shuttle with a **rocket**-fired **capsule** called Orion. It was first tested in an un-piloted flight in 2014. NASA hopes

Fun Fact

Orion is the name of a constellation. It was also the name of the Apollo 16 Lunar Module, which carried astronauts to the surface of the moon in April 1972.

crewed test flights will begin in 2018. Although Orion looks like the Apollo capsule that could carry three astronauts, Orion is much larger and more advanced. It has room for six crew members.

In addition to Orion, several private companies began building craft to carry astronauts and cargo into space, in response to a call for commercial space operations made by United States

President Barack Obama in 2010. In 2012, SpaceX became the first private company to send an unpiloted cargo vehicle to the ISS.

Above, an artist's drawing of the Orion capsule, with a cutaway view to show equipment and crew seating. At right, an Orion capsule floats in the Pacific Ocean after its successful 2014 test flight.

What Will Launch NASA's Orion Capsule into Space?

To send the Orion **capsule** to its destination in space, NASA is building a **launch vehicle** called the Space Launch System (SLS). In its final form, the SLS will be the most powerful **rocket** ever made.

Just like the Orion capsule looks like an Apollo capsule, the SLS looks a little like the big Saturn 5 rockets that blasted the Apollo **astronauts** to the moon. But the SLS will actually use the same **boosters** and rocket engines that the space shuttle used. The SLS has different sections, called *stages*, used during a flight. When a stage is used up, it separates from the rocket and falls back to Earth.

NASA plans to test the SLS in an uncrewed flight in 2018. Then, in 2023, it will send astronauts in an Orion capsule around the **moon** and back using the SLS.

After this test mission, the SLS will be ready to take astronauts anywhere in the inner **solar system.** The rocket will be able to be built in different sizes, depending on the needs of the mission. In its largest configuration, it will be able to take crews to Mars.

Highlights

- NASA's Space Launch System will launch Orion capsules into space.
- The SLS will be the most powerful rocket ever made.

The Space Launch System (SLS) is shown shortly after launch in this artist's drawing. The SLS is carrying an Orion capsule.

What Is Replacing the Space Shuttle?

Even so, each mission cost an estimated $1 billion. In the early 2000's, NASA began to worry about the age and safety of the **orbiters.**

Two shuttle missions ended in disaster. In 1986, the shuttle Challenger broke apart shortly after launch, killing all seven **astronauts** aboard. In 2003, the shuttle Columbia broke apart as it reentered Earth's **atmosphere.** All seven crew members died in this disaster, too. In 2011, NASA ended all shuttle missions.

NASA planned to replace the shuttle with a **rocket**-fired **capsule** called Orion. It was scheduled for an unpiloted test flight in 2014.

Fun Fact

Orion is the name of a constellation. It was also the name of the Apollo 16 Lunar Module, which carried astronauts to the surface of the moon in April 1972.

In addition, several private companies began building craft to carry astronauts and cargo into space, in response to a call for commercial space operations made by United States President Barack Obama in 2010.

Until then, Russia's Soyuz spacecraft was carrying U.S. astronauts to the International Space Station (ISS). Russian and Japanese cargo vehicles ferried supplies. In 2012, SpaceX became the first private company to send an unpiloted cargo vehicle to the ISS.

Highlights

- The U.S. space shuttle was the first spacecraft that was mostly reusable.
- NASA is designing a new shuttle, called Orion, which will be tested on an unpiloted flight in 2014.

To replace the space shuttle, NASA plans called for the Orion spacecraft to be carried into space by a rocket (artist's drawing, right).

NASA plans to test its new Orion spacecraft (above, in an artist's drawing) in 2014.

What Is the International Space Station?

The International Space Station

Highlights

- The International Space Station is a joint project by more than 15 nations.
- Its first two pieces were the Russian-built Zarya and U.S.-built Unity modules.
- Construction of the station in space began in 1998.

The International Space Station is a large, inhabited Earth-orbiting **satellite.** The station was constructed in **modules,** or pieces. The first module, Zarya, was built and launched by Russia in 1998. The second, Unity, was built and launched by the United States later in 1998. The space shuttles brought many modules into orbit. As modules arrived in space, **astronauts** connected them to existing modules through **extravehicular activity.**

The ISS contains over a dozen modules. All of the important modules are in place, but just as a building can be added on to after it has been completed, officials plan to add more modules to the space station in the near future. The ISS will continue to be used until at least 2020.

The space station is truly an international effort. More than 15 nations, including Canada, Russia, and the United States, are partners in the project. The joining of the Zarya and Unity modules symbolized the start of a new era in cooperation between nations, at least in space exploration.

How Do Astronauts Get to the International Space Station?

Since 2011, when the space shuttle program ended, all **astronauts** have gotten to the ISS in Russia's Soyuz spacecraft. With dozens of missions to its credit, the **capsule** is one of the most successful crewed spacecraft in history.

Designed by Russia when it was still part of the Soviet Union, Soyuz first flew in 1967. It has experienced two deadly disasters early in its history. In 1967, a **cosmonaut** died when the parachute on his capsule did not open correctly. In 1971, three cosmonauts were killed when the craft lost pressure during reentry. After both of these disasters, engineers redesigned the capsule to make it safer. Today, Soyuz is considered one of the safest ways to get into space.

Highlights

- Since 2011, all astronauts have gotten to the ISS in Russia's Soyuz spacecraft.
- Soyuz first flew in 1967. It has been constantly redesigned and upgraded.
- NASA astronauts train in Russia for months to become skilled at operating the Soyuz spacecraft.

A Soyuz spacecraft

Engineers still modify the craft based on the experiences of previous missions to make it safer and more comfortable for its crew.

A **rocket** propels Soyuz into space. The capsule can carry up to three astronauts or cosmonauts to the ISS. NASA astronauts train in Russia for months to become skilled at operating the Soyuz spacecraft. They learn the Russian language so they can speak with cosmonauts and read their training manuals.

Fun Fact

At least one Soyuz capsule is docked with the ISS at all times. It serves as a "lifeboat" for the crew. In case of an emergency on the space station, the crewmembers could escape and return to Earth in a Soyuz capsule.

What Have We Learned So Far on the International Space Station?

Ever since the first piloted space flights, scientists have studied the effects of space exposure and **microgravity** on the human body. **Astronauts** on the International Space Station (ISS) continue this research. It is even more important now that people spend months at a time in space. What we learn today may also be used on ultralong flights to other **planets.**

Astronauts on the ISS also carry out experiments with construction materials. They expose hundreds of possible future space construction materials to the environment of space. Then, samples are returned to Earth and studied. NASA hopes the results will help engineers build stronger, more durable spacecraft.

Astronauts are not the only people conducting research from the space station. A NASA program called Earth Knowledge Acquired by Middle School Students (EarthKAM) allows thousands of middle school students to photograph and study Earth, using a digital camera mounted on the ISS.

Cosmonaut Gennady Padalka measures the growth of plants in a greenhouse aboard the Zvezda module of the ISS as part of a biology experiment.

Highlights

- Scientists have tested how construction materials react to the environment of space.
- They have also measured the growth of various plants in space.
- Middle school students have also carried out experiments from the space station.

What Useful Things on Earth Were Created for the Space Program?

Many of the products people on Earth use every day are based on technology that was developed for NASA missions. For example, NASA developed the materials and technologies that are used in smoke

Highlights

- Many of the products we use today were developed by NASA scientists for use by astronauts.
- NASA technology has been used to make products in such fields as health and medicine, public safety, transportation, recreation, and computer technology.

Cordless tools were originally developed by NASA for use by the Apollo astronauts.

Technology developed by NASA has been used in such products as Tang breakfast drink, joystick controllers for video games, and ear thermometers.

European Space Agency astronaut Claude Nicollier uses a power tool during a mission to repair the Hubble Space Telescope in 1999.

detectors, ear thermometers, TV satellite dishes, joystick controllers for video games, transparent braces for teeth, and more shock-absorbent football helmets. Cordless tools also were developed by NASA to help Apollo astronauts drill for moon samples. Other NASA-related devices are being used in transportation, computer technology, and public safety.

How Can Kids Get Involved in Space Exploration?

There are many ways that young people can get involved in space exploration. Boy Scout and Girl Scout organizations offer space-exploration achievement badges. To earn the badges, scouts learn about the history of space travel, design a base for the moon or Mars, or even build and launch model **rockets.**

NASA sponsors many programs for schools. In the "Send Your Art to Space" program, kids were invited to submit a piece of art that represented their school. That art was then sent to the International Space Station.

Fun Fact

Various nations use different names for their space explorers. U.S., Canadian, Australian, and European space explorers are called astronauts; Russian explorers, cosmonauts; Chinese, taikonauts; and explorers from India, vyomanauts.

With a personal computer, you can tune into a variety of webcasts from NASA. These webcasts feature scientists, engineers, NASA managers, and **astronauts.** And during shuttle missions you can watch NASA TV on the Internet, with start-to-finish coverage from Mission Control.

Highlights

- Both Boy Scouts and Girl Scouts can earn merit badges by learning about space exploration.
- Many NASA programs allow students to play a part in specific space missions.
- Anyone with a computer can follow webcasts in which scientists and astronauts talk about their current mission.

A Cub Scout practices satellite repair on a simulator at NASA's Space Center in Houston.

Can Tourists Travel into Space?

Since the first piloted space flight in 1961, fewer than 1,000 people have flown in space. Even people who qualify as an **astronaut** are not guaranteed a mission. What other ways might there be to experience space travel and tourism in the future?

A small number of wealthy civilians have paid to travel to the International Space Station (ISS) aboard Russian spacecraft. The trips were arranged by Space Adventures, a private company. The company also offers **microgravity** training, simulated spacewalk training, and other programs.

The private British company Virgin Galactic began taking deposits in 2005 for brief flights into space on the VSS Enterprise (also called SpaceShipTwo). The company plans to start flying tourists into space soon, but a crash of VSS Enterprise during a 2014 test flight has slowed its progress.

Several other companies have developed plans for space hotels, and even hotels on the moon!

Highlights

- Fewer than 1,000 people have flown in space since the first piloted space flight in 1961.
- Several companies planned to carry tourists into space, allowing people who were not trained astronauts to experience microgravity and see Earth from space.

American multimillionaire Dennis Tito (right) enters the ISS in 2001. Tito became the first space tourist when he paid Russia a reported $20 million to fly him to the ISS aboard a Soyuz spacecraft.

SpaceShipOne, a rocket launched from an airplane, in 2004 became the first privately funded, piloted craft to reach space.

So You Want to Become a Space Explorer?

To become a NASA **astronaut,** you must have at least a bachelor's degree in engineering, science, or math. An advanced degree is even better. You also must have completed three years of related experience after graduation. Pilot astronauts must have at least 1,000 hours of experience in jet aircraft. Competition is extremely stiff. Usually, over 4,000 people apply for about 20 openings every two years.

Supporting the astronauts on every mission are thousands of other workers, in jobs ranging from research pilots to microbiologists. Requirements for these positions depend on the job.

Highlights

- To become a NASA astronaut, a candidate must have at least a bachelor's degree in engineering, science, or mathematics.

- Very few people become astronauts, and even fewer fly on a mission.

- But there are other ways students can experience being in space.

To experience a simulated space mission, some kids visit a Challenger Learning Center. About 50 centers—in Canada, South Korea, the United Kingdom, and the United States—offer scale models of mission control and an **orbiting** space station.

And for sheer fun, nothing beats space camp. At space camps in the United States, Canada, and Europe, kids may meet astronauts, try out motion and **microgravity** simulators, and design space robots.

A student tries out the cockpit of a simulated space shuttle at space camp.

Glossary

airlock On a spacecraft, the chamber between the outer door that leads to space and the door leading to the inside of the spacecraft.

astronaut A pilot or member of the crew of a spacecraft.

atmosphere The mass of gases that surrounds a planet.

booster A rocket sometimes attached to a launch vehicle to provide extra power.

capsule A section of a spacecraft that can be used or ejected as a unit.

cosmonaut A Russian astronaut.

extravehicular activity (EVA) Work or other activity outside a spacecraft.

flight deck The uppermost compartment of the cabin in a space shuttle, which contains the controls for the shuttle's guidance and navigation.

gravity The effect of a force of attraction that acts between all objects because of their mass (that is, the amount of matter the objects have).

hatch A door or opening on a spacecraft that can be sealed.

Karman Line An altitude of about 62 miles (100 kilometers) above Earth's surface (from sea level). This height has become an international boundary marking the beginning of outer space.

launch vehicle A rocket that carries a satellite or spacecraft into space.

microgravity A condition of very low gravity, especially approaching weightlessness.

module A self-contained unit in a spacecraft, designed to serve a particular function.

moon A smaller body that orbits a planet.

orbit The path that a smaller body takes around a larger body; for instance, the path that a planet takes around the sun. Also, to travel in an orbit.

orbiter In the space shuttle, a winged craft that looks like an airplane and which holds the cabin where the astronauts are.

oxygen A nonmetallic chemical element.

planet A large, round body in space that orbits a star. A planet must have sufficient gravitational pull to clear other objects from the area of its orbit.

probe An unpiloted device sent to explore space. Most probes send *data* (information) from space.

rocket A type of engine that pushes itself forward or upward by producing *thrust* (a force).

satellite A natural satellite is an object that orbits a planet or asteroid. An artificial satellite is an object built by people and launched into space, where it continuously orbits Earth or some other body. Artificial satellites are used to send weather or other scientific information back to Earth.

solar system A group of bodies in space made up of a star and the planets and other objects orbiting around the star.

ultraviolet rays An invisible form of light. The sun is the major natural source of ultraviolet rays on Earth.

For More Information

Books

Eyewitness Space Exploration by Carole Stott (DK Publishing, 2014)

Look to the Stars by Buzz Aldrin (G. P. Putnam's Sons, 2009)

Mission Control, This Is Apollo: The Story of the First Voyages to the Moon by Andrew Chaikin (Viking, 2009)

Space Exploration: Science, Technology, and Engineering by Wil Mara (Children's Press, 2015)

Websites

Curious About Astronomy? Ask an Astronomer
http://curious.astro.cornell.edu

NASA for Students
http://www.nasa.gov/audience/forstudents/index.html

NASA's Historical Archive
http://science.ksc.nasa.gov/history/history.html

Index

Aldrin, Buzz, 23
Apollo program, 14, 15, 22, 40, 42, 52, 53
Armstrong, Neil A., 20, 21, 23
astronauts, 42, 44, 50, 53; accidents involving, 11, 14, 40, 49; early, 10-11, 18-19; living conditions for, 28, 30-37; microgravity and, 16-17; moon landings by, 20-25; names for, 54; notable, 24-25; qualifications for, 58; space walks by, 20-21, 34. *See also* space exploration, human
Atlantis (space shuttle), 16
atmosphere, 4-5, 28, 35

Bluford, Guion S., Jr., 24, 25
boosters, 12, 13, 28, 29, 42
Boy Scouts, 54, 55

capsules, space, 10-11, 40, 42, 49
Challenger (space shuttle), 25, 40
Chang-Diaz, Franklin, 24
Cockrell, Kenneth D., 32
Columbia (space shuttle), 40
cosmonauts, 14, 18-21, 25, 49, 54. *See also* astronauts

Discovery (space shuttle), 13, 25, 29

Earth Knowledge Acquired by Middle School Students (program), 50
Endeavour (space shuttle), 35, 38
Explorer 1 satellite, 7
extravehicular activity, 20, 34, 47

Fincke, Edward, 34
flight decks, 28

Gagarin, Yuri, 18, 19
Garneau, Marc, 24, 25
Girl Scouts, 54
Glenn, John H., 25

Goddard, Robert H., 7
gravity, 12. *See also* microgravity

Ham (chimpanzee), 19
hatches, 11
Hubble Space Telescope, 38, 39

International Space Station (ISS), 8, 46-47; knowledge from, 26, 27, 50-51; living on, 17, 31, 33-36; travel to, 38, 48-49, 56
Internet, 54

Jemison, Mae C., 25

Karman Line, 4, 5
Kennedy, John F., 9

Laika (dog), 19
Launch and Entry Suits, 34, 35
launch vehicles, 12, 13, 42
Leonov, Alexei, 20, 21
Lu, Edward, 31
Luna 2 probe, 6

Magnus, Sandra, 17
Malenchenko, Yuri, 31
Mars, 42
Melvin, Leland, 16
Mercury spacecraft, 10, 11, 19, 30
microgravity, 16-17, 30, 32, 36, 56; research on, 26, 27, 50
Mir (space station), 39, 44, 45
Mission Control, 54
modules, 47
moon, 4, 6, 20-25, 42, 56
Musgrave, F. Story, 39

National Aeronautics and Space Administration (NASA), 11, 14, 23, 26, 28, 33, 40, 42, 49; origin of, 8; programs for kids, 50, 54, 55; technology from, 52-53. *See also* astronauts; space shuttle

Nicollier, Claude, 53

Obama, Barack, 40
orbiters, 28, 29, 40
Orion spacecraft, 40-41, 42-43
oxidizers, 12

Padalka, Gennady, 51
planets, 4, 50
probes, 6, 38

Ride, Sally K., 24
rockets, 6, 7, 23, 42, 49. *See also* boosters; launch vehicles
Russia, 8, 47, 49, 56

Salyut 1 (space station), 44
satellites, artificial, 6-7, 38, 47
Schirra, Walter M., Jr., 10
"Send Your Art to Space" program, 54
Shepard, Alan B., Jr., 19
Skylab, 26, 33, 44
Soviet Union, 6, 8-11, 14, 44, 49
Soyuz spacecraft, 40, 48-49, 57
space, meaning of, 4-5
Space Adventures, 56
Space Launch System (SLS), 42-43
space camp, 59
spacecraft: first, 10-11; meals on, 28, 30-31; microgravity on, 17; power for, 12-13; sleeping on, 36-37; staying clean on, 32-33. *See also* Soyuz spacecraft; Space Launch System (SLS); space shuttle; space stations
space exploration, human: beginning of, 6-7, 18-19; experiments during, 26-27; rivalry in, 8-9; technology from, 52-54; tourism and, 56-57; young people and, 26, 50, 54-55. *See also* astronauts

Spacelab, 26
space race, 8-9
SpaceShipOne, 57
space shuttle, 13, 26, 38; inspecting, 15; living on, 32-37; parts of, 28-29; replacement for, 40-41, 42-43; uses for, 38-39, 47. *See also* by name, *for example, Challenger.*
space sickness, 17
space stations, 44-45. *See also* International Space Station (ISS)
SpaceX, 40
spider webs, 27
Sputnik 1, 6, 8, 9
Sputnik 2, 19

Tereshkova, Valentina, 24, 25
Thomas, Andy, 24
Tito, Dennis, 57
Titov, Gherman, 25
tools, cordless, 52, 53

ultraviolet rays, 14
Unity module, 38, 47

Van Allen, James, 7
Vanguard 1 satellite, 6, 7
van Hoften, James D., 27
Virgin Galactic, 56
von Braun, Wernher, 7
Vostok spacecraft, 10, 11, 25
VSS Enterprise (spacecraft), 56

Whitson, Peggy, 36
Williams, Sunita, 33

Yurchikhin, Fyodor, 33

Zarya module, 47
zero gravity. *See* microgravity